ROBIN HOOD RAPS

illustrated by Martin Chatterton

 ORCHARD BOOKS

To Ann Fairbairn

and the children of Nottingham

T.M.

ORCHARD BOOKS
96 Leonard Street, London EC2A 4XD
Orchard Books Australia
14 Mars Road, Lane Cove, NSW 2066
First published in Great Britain in 2000
First paperback edition 2000
Text © Tony Mitton 2000
Illustrations © Martin Chatterton 2000
The rights of Tony Mitton to be identified as the author
and Martin Chatterton as the illustrator of this work
have been asserted by them in accordance with the
Copyright, Designs and Patents Act, 1988.
A CIP catalogue record for this book is available
from the British Library.
ISBN 1 84121 155 9 (hardback)
ISBN 1 184121 157 5 (paperback)
1 3 5 7 9 10 8 6 4 2 (hardback)
1 3 5 7 9 10 8 6 4 2 (paperback)
Printed in Great Britain

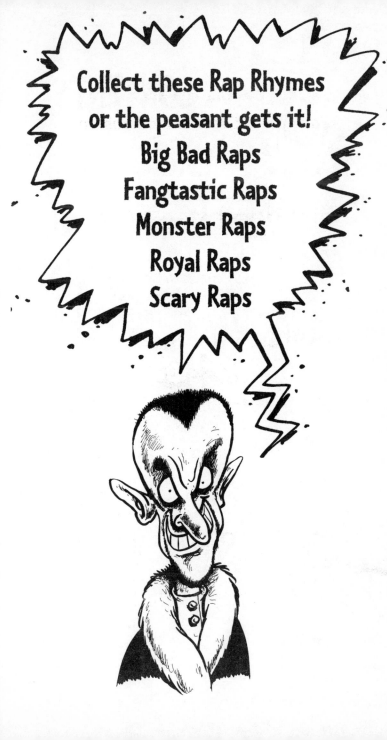

CONTENTS

Robin Hood Gets a Gang

Deep in the heart
of an old green wood
lived a guy with a bow
called Robin Hood.

And with that bow
he was quite an ace.
He could shoot a pimple
off your face.

Or better still,
from a hundred paces,
cut clean through
a pair of braces!

Now Robin Hood
was really a toff
but he had to take
his fine robes off.
For the Sheriff of Nottingham
came one day
and took his house
and land away.

The Sheriff was greedy,
mean and bad.
He took everything
the poor folk had.

And Robin had tried
to make him stop,
which made the Sheriff
shout and hop.
"You say the poor
are friends to you?
Well, OK, Robin,
be poor too!"

It wasn't fair,
it wasn't right,
but Robin couldn't
fuss or fight,
'cos the Sheriff's men
were mean and many,
while poor old Robin
didn't have any.

9

So he went to hide
in the big, wild wood,
where he learned to live
as best he could.

He set up home
in a forest den
and he gathered a gang
of merry men.

They roamed around
and broke the law,
but only so's
to help the poor.
To save them from
the Norman lash,
and give them food
and clothes and cash.

11

The Normans were
the Sheriff's thugs.
They had hard hats
and ugly mugs.
They clanked about
in chain-mail suits,
those bully boys
in metal boots.

They nicked the peasants'
nosh, in sacks.
They stole their dosh
and called it "Tax".

So Robin's gang
all firmly swore
that with those Normans
there'd be war.

They robbed the Normans
of their riches,
then pushed them into
muddy ditches.
They stripped them of
their jewels and dosh,
then shoved them backwards...
Aaaaah! SPER-LOSH!

The Sheriff scowled
and made a scene.
"I'll get those rascals
dressed in green!
I'll catch that Robin
and his band."
And he sat in a sulk,
and schemed and planned.

Robin Meets a Maid

Now this young maid
we're meeting now,
when Robin saw her
he said, "Wow!
Ain't she gorgeous?
Ain't she fine?
I hope one day
that she'll be mine."

Lady Marian
was her name,
but being a lady
wasn't her game.

Her dad was a fine
and fancy lord,
but castle life
had left her bored.

To sit and sew
just wasn't fun.
She wanted to fight
and ride and run.
So she ran away
to live in the wood.
That's how she met with
Robin Hood.

She looked just like
a fair young maid,
but she went with Robin
on many a raid.
She fought with a sword.
She twanged her bow.
And when she rode
she could really go!

She could shoot an arrow
and win the prize.
(And *oooh!* you should've
seen her eyes...)
She could fight with a staff
and give you a thump.
(And she also made
your heart go bump...)

When she met Robin
their eyes went POP!
And both their hearts
began to hop.

Robin Wrestles with a Roly Poly Priest

When Robin met Tuck
they were by a river.
The water made Robin
shudder and shiver.

Robin paid Tuck
to carry him across.
The friar said, "Money?
OK, Boss.

Money buys burgers,
beer and chips.
Just perch yourself
on my big hips.
I'll take you across
by piggyback,
then spend the fare
on a take-away snack."

But Tuck asked Robin
for too much cash.
They started to fight
and then, with a *splash*,
they both fell over,
and yes, you bet,
they both got mad
and they both got wet.

Said Tuck,

Said Robin,

And so they wrestled
and traded blows
till water got up
Robin's nose.
And Tuck began
to wail and cry,
"Not fair. There's water
in my eye!"

So in the end
they made it up,
and they both sat down
to slurp and sup.

Soon they were getting
on just fine.
(They were greatly helped
by Tuck's best wine.)
For a simple friar
and a holy priest,
he was ever so fond
of a darn good feast.

But though he was greedy,
big and fat,
he was strong as an ox
and quick as a cat.

For if he whirled
his staff around
he could knock four Normans
to the ground.

He could pick one up
on each strong arm
and still stay cool,
completely calm...
and then he'd bang
their heads together
and leave them sprawling
in the heather.

Being a priest,
he'd say, "Amen,"
then pick up the others
and do it again.

He helped the gang
to rob more dosh.
He brewed good beer
and he stewed good nosh.
And the gang all said,
"Well, here's good luck.
Let's drink a toast
to Friar Tuck!"

A Jolly Giant Joins the Merry Men

Little John was
very tall.
He made the others
look quite small.

27

He had an enormous
quarterstaff
and an even bigger
giant's laugh.
With his *Ho! Ho! Ho!*
the greenwoods rang,
and the squirrels scarpered
whenever he sang.

And when he whistled,
a gale-force breeze
would blow the branches
off the trees!

He came from far
across the land
to join with Robin
and his band.

But when they met,
at the very first sight,
they stood on a bridge
and had a fight.
The two had never
met before,
so John didn't know
who it was he saw.

The bridge was just
a narrow log,
so John said, "Gangway!
Back, you dog!
This bridge ain't wide
enough for two.
I got here first,
so back off. Shoo!"

But Robin said, "No,
you great big lout.
This staff of mine
could knock you out.
So just step back,
I'm coming through.
I don't back down
for dudes like you..."

John knocked Robin
into the stream.
That icy water
made him scream.

So Robin got out
and knocked John in,
and then they made
one helluva din.

But icy water
makes you cool.
Soon Robin said, "Friend,
I've been a fool."
And John said, "Yeah,
let's make it up.
Let's cook some deer
and share a cup."

And with those words,
from that day on,
Robin was pals
with Little John.

Robin Shames the Sheriff

Back in the heart
of Nottingham town,
sat the mean old Sheriff
with his nasty frown.
He sent his soldiers
again and again
to bring back Robin
and his merry men.

But Robin's band
were brave and good,
and furthermore
they knew the wood.
So they blew their horns,
made lots of sound,
while the soldiers galloped
round and round.

And Robin and his men
sat up in the trees
trying not to giggle
and snigger and sneeze.

So the Sheriff himself
set out from Nottingham
to have a go
at trailing and spotting 'em.
Off he went
with his sword in his hand,
peering about
for the merry band.

But the Sheriff was slow
and a little bit dim,
and the merry men
soon spotted *him*.
They stole his sword,
and, what was worse,
they helped themselves
to his big, fat purse.
(That made the Sheriff
stamp and curse!)

But the thing that really
turned him blue,
was Friar Tuck took
his sweeties too!

Then they sent him trotting
down the track
as he fumed and furied,
"I'll be back!
I'll beat the heather
and scour the wood,
and I'll stop your forest fun
for good!"

And that was how
it went from then:
Sheriff versus
Merry Men.

Prince John Pinches the Throne

The Sheriff's boss
was Bad Prince John.
He pinched the throne
to sit upon.
The real king, Richard,
was abroad,
fighting wars
with shield and sword.

He'd asked his brother,
Bad Prince John,
to rule the land
while he was gone.
But John thought,

That wicked prince
was really mean.
He stomped around
and made a scene.

He liked to hear folk
whine and wail.
He loved to lock them
up in jail.
He ordered tax
to pinch their pay.
He took the children's
toys away.

And people hated
him like mad.
That's why they called him
John the Bad.

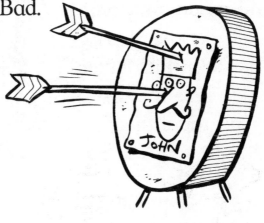

But Robin Hood said,
"Hey! Hang on!
Our real king's
not dead and gone.
He's fighting battles,
on his horse,
but he is still
our king, of course."

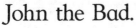

Said John, "This Robin
guy's a pain.
I'll see him off.
He hurts my brain.
I'll get the Sheriff
to keep him quiet.
He puts me off
my royal diet."

And so he sent off
lots of men
to flush the outlaws
from their den.

And that's why Robin
wore a hood
and stayed in hiding
in the wood,
and waited for
King Rick's return,
while Bad Prince John
got really stern.

43

King Richard Returns

But now it's time
to take a pause,
'cos Richard's come back
from the wars.
And people cheer
and dance and sing,
as once more Richard
is their king!

He goes to check out
Bad Prince John
and says, "Who let you
put that on?
That crown you've got
goes on *my* head.
You'll only get it
when I'm dead.

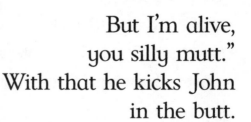

But I'm alive,
you silly mutt."
With that he kicks John
in the butt.

And when he feels
that iron shoe,
Prince John can only
say, "Boo-hoo!"
He runs right back
to Nottingham town,
where the Sheriff tries
to calm him down.

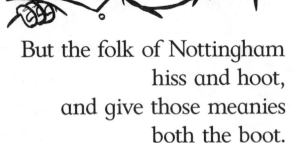

But the folk of Nottingham
hiss and hoot,
and give those meanies
both the boot.

The two turn tail.
They've had their fun.
So watch those rotters
as they run.

But now, for Britain's
best and brave,
let's hold a woodland
wedding rave,
where Marian marries
Robin Hood
and everyone's
OK for good.

Hey, look! Here comes
old Friar Tuck
to pour champagne
and wish good luck!
So lay aside
your sword and bow
and shout with me,
"For Robin, YO!"